Nature's Children

PUFFINS

Elizabeth MacLeod

Grolier

FACTS IN BRIEF

Classification of Puffins

Class: *Aves* (birds)

Order: *Charadriiformes* (birds that live in ravines or cliffs)

Family: *Alcidae* (auk)

Genus: *Fratercula, Lunda*

Species: *Fratercula arctica* (Common Puffin)

Fratercula corniculata (Horned Puffin)

Lunda cirrhata (Tufted Puffin)

World distribution. North Pacific and North Atlantic oceans.

Habitat. Oceans, coastlines and islands.

Distinctive physical characteristics. Most have a black back and head with a white chest and cheeks. The triangular bill is brightly colored during the breeding season as are the legs and feet. Each foot has three toes, which are webbed.

Habits. Puffins are excellent swimmers. They winter on the ocean and return to rocky coasts or islands to breed in the spring.

Diet. Small fish, crustaceans and plankton.

Published originally as
"Getting to Know . . . Nature's Children."

This series is approved and recommended by the Federation of Ontario Naturalists.

This library reinforced edition is available exclusively from:

Grolier Educational Corporation
Sherman Turnpike, Danbury, Connecticut 06816

ISBN 0-7172-2656-5

Contents

What looks like a cross between a penguin and a parrot? If you guessed a puffin, you're right. With their black and white feathers and colorful triangular beaks puffins are very unusual-looking birds. Although you might laugh if you saw them waddling upright on land, you would be astonished at how graceful and powerful they are swimming underwater.

Some people call puffins sea parrots or bottlenoses, but whatever you know them as, they are incredible birds. For instance, did you know that a puffin has its brightly colored beak for only a few months of the year? Or that most puffins prefer to nest underground?

To find out more about these special birds, read on.

A Family of Divers

Puffins are members of the auk family, a group of diving sea birds with short tails and necks. Birds in this family are strong swimmers, and include auklets, murres, guillemots and razorbills, as well as the Great Auk — a large flightless bird that is now extinct. A puffin's more distant cousins are sandpipers, gulls and plovers. Even though puffins look like small penguins, they're not related.

If you compare a puffin's foot — or the foot of any bird in the same family — to just about any other bird's foot, you'll see that they look different. Birds in the auk family have only three toes, whereas most birds have a fourth toe that faces backwards. This is just one of the things that sets puffins apart.

A Common, or Atlantic Puffin.

Three's Company

There are three kinds of puffins. At first glance you might think that they are all quite similar, but take a closer look and you'll see that it's not all that difficult to tell them apart.

The Common, or Atlantic, Puffin is probably the one that you've seen most often in photographs. It has a big bright bill, a black back and white chest feathers. It's the smallest of the three puffins and it nests on coastlines along the Atlantic Ocean, from Greenland down to northern Maine in the United States. It can also be found on the coasts of Iceland, Ireland, France and along the north coast of the Soviet Union.

The biggest puffin is the Tufted Puffin. Even though it's the largest, it only weighs a little more than a loaf of bread and stands about as high as your knee. It gets its name from the tufts of yellow feathers on the sides of its head. These tufts look quite handsome as they stream out behind the puffin when it flies. However, when the Tufted Puffin is perched on a rock, the wind can blow the long feathers all over its face, making it difficult for the poor bird to see. You'll find this puffin along the Pacific coastline from Alaska to California, as well as in Japan.

The Horned Puffin is the middle-sized puffin. If you notice the fleshy "horn" by its eye, you'll know how it gets its name. It nests on the west coast of North America and the east coast of Asia.

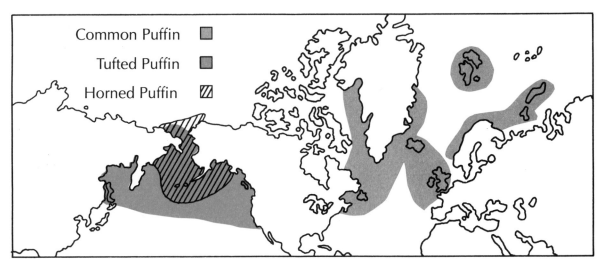

Where puffins nest and feed.

Below the Waves

Puffins are expert divers and swimmers. They don't look very dynamic as they bob along the ocean's surface, but the instant they spot a school of fish far below, they flick their wings open and go into action. With just one powerful stroke and a back kick, they're underwater. Then they partially fold back their wings and use them as propellers. Like penguins, puffins seem to fly, not swim, through the water. They zoom along just as most birds move through the air. To glide, a puffin simply pulls its wings in close to its body.

Notice how streamlined this puffin looks whizzing through the water.

Fish Lovers

Puffins dine upon crab, plankton, squid and fish, with smelt, herring, cod and sand eels being their favorites.

You may have seen a picture of a puffin with a beak filled with fish. Just how does it manage to fit as many as 40 small fish in its beak at the same time? By catching them in a special way.

As this fabulous fisherman swims underwater through a school of fish, it moves its head from side to side. This allows the puffin to stack the fish one at a time crosswise in its bill. Tiny spines on its tongue and the upper part of its beak hold the catch firmly in place. Once its beak is filled, the puffin flies up out of the water to a nearby cliff or island to feed its young.

When a puffin is dining alone, it doesn't stack fish. Instead it simply eats them as it catches them.

A beakful of fish to feed its offspring.

Eye Spy

Have you ever noticed how difficult it is for you to see things clearly when you dive underwater? That's because your eyes are designed to see well in air. Since you don't spend a lot of time underwater, it's not important that you see well there. But puffins have to be eagle-eyed in air and in water.

Fortunately, puffins — like all birds — have an extra set of eyelids. The middle part of these eyelids is clear, and the puffin simply flicks them across its eyes when it dives underwater. The eyelids act like goggles keeping the water from blurring the puffin's vision and enabling it to spot a likely meal.

The fleshy "horn" of this Horned Puffin makes its eyes appear larger than they really are.

Waterproof Feathers

A puffin depends on its brilliant black and white feathers to keep it warm and dry, no matter how long it stays underwater. To keep its coat in shape it spends a lot of time preening.

First the puffin ruffles its feathers and removes any damaged ones. Then it spreads oil from a gland near its tail all over its feathers. The oil provides a waterproof coating and also helps to keep the feathers properly arranged. Hooks or barbs on the feathers lock them together, making the puffin as streamlined as possible so that it can fly through the air or swim through the water smoothly.

Taking off with a lot of splashing.

Up, Up and Away

Puffins are fairly good fliers but they do have trouble with their take-offs and landings. Because of their relatively small wings and chunky bodies, they have to beat their wings very fast to lift off. Sometimes if they're taking off from the water, they end up crashing headfirst into the waves. Luckily puffins are so tough that they bob up safely or bounce into the air. Taking off is a lot easier if they launch themselves from cliffs.

When it's time to land a puffin seems to have very little control. To slow down, it spreads it feet in front of itself and flares its tail. It also helps if the bird can touch down with the wind blowing into its face. However, unlike most birds which coast to a stop, puffins appear to just drop in. When they land on water you'll even hear a loud plop. On land, any puffins standing around watch nervously and get ready to scatter when another comes in for a landing.

Three, two, one . . . blast-off!

Brrr!

Imagine going through the whole winter floating about on the cold ocean, spending your days diving and dozing. That's what puffins seem to do. From approximately September to March each year they swim about catching fish, usually with only a few other puffins for company.

Actually, scientists aren't absolutely sure what puffins do all winter or exactly where they go. Most experts think that the birds scatter widely over the ocean and never come ashore at all during the winter months. Some may spend the cold months very close to their summer nesting grounds, while others may migrate long distances. Wherever they do go, they are rarely within sight of land for the entire winter.

A Tufted Puffin.

Creaks, Purrs and Gurgles

A puffin makes a lot of different sounds. If it wants to threaten another puffin — or some other bird — it lets out a short, harsh *urrr* sound. It also communicates by making a deep, purring *arrr* and a short *haa-haa* laugh. While sitting on its egg, a parent may make a long call that sounds like *haa-aa-aa-aa*.

Puffins also get their point across without making any noise at all. They greet one another by standing face to face, with one's bill on top of the other's, and pushing back and forth like a seesaw. A big, wide-mouthed yawn tells other puffins to stay away. Sometimes this yawn follows a sound like a rusty hinge creaking or a gurgle.

When two puffins get into a fight, they growl, trying to scare each other off. If that doesn't work, one will grab the other's jaw with its bill, then the two roll about, slashing with their wings and feet. They can become so involved in their fight that they may even roll over the edge of a cliff!

"Are you friend or foe?"

Look Out!

Puffins nest on islands or on rocky cliffs overlooking the sea. Although there aren't many other animals in these places, they still have to be on the lookout for predators. Ravens, gulls, peregrine falcons, crows and eagles all hunt puffins, and puffins that nest in northern areas have to beware of snowy owls as well. Most of these birds will also steal food from adult puffins and try to fly off with eggs or chicks. Foxes, river otters and rats can also be a danger since they consider puffin eggs a tasty treat.

Waiting for the fog to lift.

All Together

Puffins nest in large groups known as colonies. There may be as many as 50 000 birds in a single colony. Horned Puffins and Tufted Puffins sometimes nest in the same areas and compete with each other for burrows. Other birds, such as petrels, terns and guillemots, may also share the same locations.

No matter how closely packed together puffins are, they defend their tiny territories fiercely, and the colonies can become very noisy as the birds squawk and scream at one another. Living in a group has its advantages, however. For instance, it's easy to find out where the fish are just by watching where the other birds are having luck fishing.

Busy Beak

Puffins' beaks are useful for a lot more than just catching and carrying food. During the mating season they come in handy as shovels or chisels to dig burrows in hard earth. And they can also be used as pliers to remove rocks from burrows. Sometimes these rocks weigh twice as much as the puffin!

Puffins also use their beaks to attract a mate. Most of the year the beak is small and a dull gray-brown color. During the breeding season, however, the bill grows a brightly colored sheath that makes it twice its usual size.

After the mating season, this brilliant sheath falls off in sections. The Tufted Puffin, for example, drops its beak cover in seven pieces.

The bright colors of this puffin's beak will surely help it to attract a mate.

Paddles and Diggers

Puffins have an amazing number of uses for their big webbed feet. Naturally, they use them to scramble over the rocky shores where they nest and to paddle as they float on the ocean's waves. They also use them to steer when they dive deep underwater, and to help dig their burrows.

Each toe ends in a sharp claw which helps the puffin grab on and keep its balance as it climbs over rocks and stones. A strong, curved, sharp inner toenail on each foot works as a pick to help the bird dig in the hard, rocky soil where it makes its nest. And the webbing between its toes makes it easy for the puffin to toss the soil out behind it as it works.

Puffin foot showing claws.

Just like the puffin's beak, its feet become very colorful during the mating season. They turn from brownish-green to bright red to help the puffin look its best to attract a mate.

Mating Time

By the time the mating season comes around, both the male and female puffins have grown their large, colorful beaks and their feet have become brightly colored as well. Puffin courtship takes place on land and in the water. It usually begins on a cliff when a young male spots an unattached young female. He walks over to her and nibbles lightly at her bill. If she's interested she stands facing him, chest to chest, and they shake their heads rapidly so that their bills clash. Afterwards they may run around each other, then crouch and nuzzle each other's bill. Then they take to the sea, calling and diving and rubbing bills.

Courtship is very important to puffins because they usually mate for life. The courtship process lasts from two to seven days, during which the birds nuzzle each other's throats and chest feathers, nod their heads and give their mating call. The male may also open his mouth and display the brightly colored insides.

"Back off – this is our territory!"

Home Sweet Home

Once a puffin has chosen a mate, the pair finds a suitable spot to nest. Older puffins may return to the same nest year after year. A new pair will try to find a burrow that was dug by some other bird, or by a rabbit. If necessary, they'll dig their own.

The nest is a tunnel about a metre (3 feet) long, often curved down to about 30 centimetres (a foot) below the surface. Burrows may be connected underground, but each one has a private entrance and a nest chamber at the end of the tunnel. Sometimes a burrow will have two "tenants" since other seabirds, such as razorbills or guillemots, may nest just inside the entrance to the tunnel.

The puffins carry grass, seaweed and feathers into the nest burrow and drop the materials anywhere in the passageway. There's no proper lining to soften the inside of the rocky tunnel or protect the egg that will soon be laid there.

A little foliage to make the burrow more homey.

Countdown

The female puffin usually lays one egg. She may lay a second egg later if something happens to the first one. The egg is white with light purple or brown spots at its large end. Both parents take turns sitting on the egg and since it's fairly big, the parent has to tuck it under one wing and lean his or her body on it to keep it warm. Both parents have special spots under each wing just for incubating eggs.

The parents take turns keeping the egg warm, although the female does most of the work. She spends long periods on the egg, usually changing places with her mate for a while at night. By the beginning of July, about 42 days after it was laid, the egg is ready to hatch.

Guarding the entrance to a burrow.

Welcome to the World

It takes the baby puffin about four days to break out of its shell. When it finally emerges, the baby is covered in soft down and doesn't look much like its parents at all. For the first few days the parents stay with the hatchling almost continually and take turns catching fish for it.

The chick starts right off eating small fish without needing to have them predigested by its parents. It can eat its entire weight in fish each day, and the parents make as many as eight flights a day to get it food. During the 40 to 45 days the chick stays in the burrow, it may consume up to 2000 fish!

This fluffy puffball doesn't look the least bit like its parents.

A Jump in the Dark

By the time the baby puffin is about six weeks old it looks quite similar to its parents, although its bill is small and dark and its wings are not yet fully developed. At this point its mom and dad leave it and return to the water. Their feathers are ready to molt and they will be unable to fly for several weeks until their new feathers grow in. They are therefore no longer able to carry fish from the ocean to the cliff for their offspring.

The chick may sit in the burrow for up to a week waiting for its parents to return. Finally, once its flight feathers have grown in, it decides it's ready to find out what's outside the tunnel.

Chicks usually leave their nests at night, which is a good thing because that makes it more difficult for enemies to spot them. The little puffins tumble over the sides of the cliffs to the water below. Don't worry, they're very light and fluffy, and they always land safely. After a quick shake of their feathers they're soon swimming. They seem to know instinctively how to dive for food, and in a few days they begin to fly.

Opposite page:
The world beyond the burrow can be a frightening place.

All Grown Up

Scientists can't seem to agree on whether young puffins find their parents in the ocean and spend the winter with them or not. It seems unlikely. What we do know is that the youngsters remain on the ocean for two years and don't head back to land until their second or third summer. Talk about a lot of swimming!

At the age of about three the young puffin arrives at the breeding spot early and tries to find a mate and a burrow. It may not succeed for another year or two, however. By that time it is a full-grown puffin and has learned everything it needs to know to raise a family. With a little luck, it may live for another 15 years in the northern oceans of the world.

Time to return to the sea for winter.

Words to Know

Breeding season   The time of year during which animals come together to produce young.

Chick   A young bird before or after hatching.

Colony   Name given to the large groups in which puffins nest.

Down   Short, soft feathers that cover young birds or underlie the outer feathers of adult birds.

Hatch   To emerge from an egg.

Hatchling   A chick that is breaking out or has just broken out of the egg.

Migrate   To move from one place to another regularly, according to the season.

Molt   To shed feathers, skin, shell or horns periodically before a new growth.

Plankton   Very small animal or plant life that lives near the surface of salt and fresh water.

Predator   An animal that hunts other animals for food.

Preening   Cleaning and oiling the feathers.

Smelt   Small green and silver fish.

Territory   Area that an animal or group of animals lives in and often defends from other animals of the same kind.

INDEX

Cover Photo: A. Petretti (WWF–Photolibrary)

Photo Credits: Breck P. Kent, pages 4, 13, 34-35; Brenda Tharp, pages 6, 30; New York Zoological Society, page 10; Derek Kirkland (Network Stock Photo File), page 14; Barry Griffiths (Network Stock Photo File), pages 17, 26, 29, 33, 38; Cynthia and Amor Klotzbach, pages 18, 45; Boyd Norton, page 21; G. Ziesler (Peter Arnold, Inc.), page 23; G.C. Kelley, pages 24, 42; Phyllis Greenberg, pages 37, 46; Bruno J. Zehnder (Peter Arnold, Inc.), page 41.